EGYPT

STORIES FROM THE MISSION FIELD

EGYPT

STORIES FROM THE MISSION FIELD

ST SHENOUDA PRESS
SYDNEY, AUSTRALIA
2023

EGYPT

Stories from the Mission Field

COPYRIGHT © 2023
St Shenouda Press

All rights reserved. Except for brief quotations in critical publications or reviews, no part of this book may be reproduced in any manner without prior written permission from the publisher.

ST SHENOUDA PRESS
8419 Putty Rd,
Putty, NSW, 2330
Sydney, Australia

www.stshenoudamonastery.org.au

ISBN 13: 978-0-6457703-6-0

All scripture quotations, unless otherwise indicated, are taken from the New King James Version®. Copyright © 1982 by Thomas Nelson, Inc. Used by permission. All rights reserved.

Cover Design:
Mariana Hanna
In and Out Creation Pty Ltd
inandoutcreations.com.au

Contents

Introduction	7
The Unplanned Visit: Fr. Kyrillos Farag	9
A Scene from Heaven: Anonymous	15
The Voice of an Angel and a Heart Made to Love All: Marissa Gendy	19
The Bracelet That I Will Always Cherish: Ameer Zaki	25
It Was A Surprise To All Of Us: Anne Joseph	31
The Most Generous Love: Marina Sawires	33
A Faith Truly Unshaken: Youanaa Gendy	43
The Day God Hugged Me: Marena Soliman	49
Encountering Christ: Marina Fahim	55
A Life Changing Experience: Anonymous	65
The Healing Crosses: Anonymous	75
Beyond My Wildest Imagination: Yostina Boktor	79
An Apple a Day Keeps the Devil Away: Maria Gindy	89
Boundless Faith: David Morkos	93

Introduction

'Egypt: Stories From the Mission Field' invites the readers on a captivating journey through the experiences of various members of the Body of Christ from all over the world who embraced the call to serve in this culturally rich and spiritually profound region.

From the bustling villages along the Nile to the serene monastic settlements in the desert, each story paints a vivid picture of the challenges and unveils the acts of fellowship, love, hope, simplicity and spiritual encounters experienced by the youth.

In these inspiring stories, the profound mystery of "Love" is beautifully translated into tangible actions. The book aims to awaken a deep sense of compassion within readers and ignite a passion for service. It seeks to inspire the readers to embrace their unique call to serve others, recognizing that true fulfillment lies in selflessly giving of oneself following in the footsteps of Christ. The stories within the book exemplify that Christ does not solely call those who are already qualified, but rather, through His grace, He qualifies those who respond to His call.

The Unplanned Visit

- Fr. Kyrillos Farag -

One day we went to serve 'Ekhwat El Rab' (those in need) in a village in El Minya. When we arrived there, they told us about a lady named 'Mabsoota' (happy). When we went to meet this lady, we found that she was a happy and joyful woman. It was unbelievable. From the moment we entered the home, we immediately noticed the massive smile on her face and her hearty laugh. Her laugh could remove any form of sadness from your heart. Her demeanor caused us to briefly forget that we were visiting a poverty-stricken area in Egypt. It would have been easy to assume that she was living a really great life. However, her life was extremely difficult. She was married to an incredibly ill husband named Hany*. Despite his illness, Hany was also really joyful. Mabsoota and Hany have a total of 5 children. All 5 of these children have brain related illnesses. They have paralysis in their muscles. This type of illness appears in children at age 12 and generally causes death by age 17. It is an auto-immune disease and any attempt to cure this disease is extremely costly. This poor family was living in a one bedroom unit, struggling to acquire basic necessities like food. When we arrived, Mabsoota shared with us about her family and some of her life experiences. She shared that her children had onset of this disease at the age of 12, and eventually they would not be able to move as it would paralyze their muscles. Every day she had to pick them up, bathe them, clean up after them and take them to the bathroom. She would always pray to God about them and she felt God saying to her "this is how I want them for Me." Because of this, she was not saddened about their state. She was always thanking God for her life and she would always say "He loves me, and He doesn't love anyone else in the world as much as He loves me." She would say this quite often. From the amount of love in her heart came an outpouring of thankfulness. The gratitude in her heart was unbelievable. She has lost 3 kids at the hands of this illness, and after our visitation to her, we heard that her husband passed away as well. And yet, she is still faithful in her joy and gratitude towards God. If these circumstances were our own, we would be in deep sorrow and depression. Mabsoota was the complete opposite. The joy that radiated from her face and her constant words of thanksgiving made her a really special and extraordinary woman. Mabsoota also explained to us that she doesn't look at the situations here on earth, but that she always looks to life in Heaven with Christ. Even though her family is sick here on Earth, she knows that there will be a day when all of us will be joined together in Heaven, joyful and happy. Despite her incredibly simple lifestyle and her difficult life conditions, she had profound faith in God. The joy that she was carrying is impossible to find here on Earth. It had to have come from Christ.

Sometimes I meet people who live back home in Australia, with really wonderful living conditions and the latest version of everything (clothes, cars, phones, food), but these people still lack the joy that Mabsoota was radiating. Everyone who visits Mabsoota, leaves 'mabsoot' (happy). When we visited her, everyone that was in my visitation group insisted on taking a photo with her one on one, so that they would never forget this blessed woman, her joyful and peaceful face, and how much she touched all of our hearts. She was so happy that she could witness Christ's love to us.

† † †

Another home visitation showed me how God truly looks after His children, especially the extremely poor, even if they don't realize this. One day we were visiting a village in Kora Saeed. We always split into groups on visitations and each group would go do a house visitation separately so that we could visit as many homes as possible. I went on home visitations with a youth named Joseph*. He and I had 18 houses to visit.

In every house we entered, we sat down with the family, read the Bible and prayed. Then we would discuss what items they needed for their homes and we inspected the property to see if there was any support we could provide them. Sometimes this meant trying to fix a broken roof, or repair a light bulb. If there were any sick people in the home, we would pray for them. If there was anyone trying to find a job, we would try and connect them with people and opportunities. There were some people who wanted to learn and earn an education. Other people needed to go to the hospital for surgeries. So it took us a long time to complete each visitation due to the nature of the conversations and requests that took place. At every house, before leaving, we would leave them with a sum of money. On one particular day I was really tired. I had the flu and the dirt in the air in Saeed in Egypt was making it particularly difficult for me to breathe. Once we finished the final visitation, we went back into the microbus where I leaned my head against the window and fell asleep from the exhaustion. I was then woken up by one of the youth telling me "Abouna, there is a house that wasn't visited." I told him I checked the list and made sure we visited every home. He replied "no, this is a new one that just came to our attention." There was a woman following one of the other visitation groups pleading with them to visit her home because her husband was unwell. The youth requested that we please go visit her as well. We agreed and a group of us left the bus and walked for a bit until we found her unit. It was on the second floor. Upon entering the unit we found a family consisting of a father, a mother, 4 children, a grandfather and grandmother, and one of the mothers' sisters with all of her children. They were all sitting in a room that was no bigger than 8 meters. The father was the main financial supporter of the family, and he had been recently diagnosed with renal failure. This is really common in Egypt. It is the result of drinking unclean water. With this disease patients also get anemia, and anemia makes them very weak. The anemia prevented the father from working. Because the father was not working, nobody in that family of over ten people had a source of income. He worked as a laborer moving cement around, building things and performing farming work among other things. Because he could not do his work, the whole family was impacted. I will never forget how he looked when we saw him. He was sleeping in his bed and looked very weak, and he lacked the energy to move. I sat next to him on the bed, and then I began to sing in Arabic to him the hymn with the words that read: "Don't ever think that I have forgotten you. My son, don't worry. Be at peace." The man started crying when he heard us singing this hymn. We then asked what they needed from us, and they said that this father needed a blood transfusion of 3.5 liters of blood. The family didn't have any money for this transfusion. At that time, the cost of this was approximately 5000 pounds. By that point in the evening we had given out all the money that we had during our other visitations and we didn't have much left. We excused ourselves and walked outside, and as a group we started counting how much money we had in our pockets or wallets. When we counted what we had, we found that it was exactly

5,000 pounds. We gave the family the 5,000 pounds that they were praying for and told the man to rest assured because he would receive the blood transfusion. After that we put him on a program for renal dialysis.

This man wasn't on our initial schedule to visit. We were not supposed to go see him in his home. We were about to go home on a microbus headed back to Cairo. We weren't anticipating another visitation and all of the groups had given out the majority of the money allocated to visitations. But, there is beauty in the way that God paused our plans, and sent us to this man, out of our schedule. A man whose circumstances and family nobody knew anything of. And all of the leftover money with the whole group was the exact amount of money that this man needed. It was also beautiful how God sent us to send joy to this man and give him hope. We entered their home which was filled with a deep sense of worry and sadness, but we left their home filled with joy and laughter. They were singing and praying. This is the beauty of serving the needy in Egypt. We see God's hand working in unexplainable ways and we see His love expressed through these services.

*For the sake of privacy, the names of the individuals in the story have been changed to Hany and Joseph, appearing throughout the stories in this order.

A Scene from Heaven

- Anonymous -

I served in the Serve to Learn program with Coptic Orphans in 2023. As part of the service trip, we would visit the children's homes in the evenings after teaching classes during the day. At their homes, we'd sit with the children and their family members, chat with them, play with them, and pray with them. There was one home in particular that was the most special home visitation for me. I can't explain it but the time we spent together felt especially blessed.

We visited that house with a volunteer representative, and it felt like a moment when time stopped. We were no longer there to serve anyone, but simply to enjoy each other's company. It was a scene from heaven: there was so much joy, so much laughter, so much friendship, as we sat around the table playing a game of 'cheat' with a deck of cards.

We were all jokingly accusing one another of cheating, even though that was precisely the point of the game! It did not feel like we had just met minutes ago, but that we had known each other for ages as longtime friends and family- though I really believe we became a spiritual family that day. As I looked around the table at everyone laughing their hearts out with each other, I felt that this was a glimpse of what the Kingdom of Heaven will be like: a simple and joyful banquet of celebration with loved ones.

At the end of the visit, I ended up being the one who prayed. This was one of the few houses in which I did this. It was a struggle to pray in Arabic but it was still a genuine prayer from my heart. It went something like this: "Thank you God for the wonderful time we spent together. Please always help these children and bring joy to their hearts." Not only did the family help me say the words to pray when I stuttered and struggled to find the right ones, but they also wholeheartedly agreed to my prayer saying "Ameen Ya Rab" when I finished. That's why I believe it was especially powerful (Matthew 18:19).

That little girl in the home was very devastated that we were not going to see each other again after the service ended, and truthfully so was I. But I told her that if we kept praying for each other, our prayers would connect us until we see each other again, whether that was on earth or in heaven. I don't even really understand where I had gotten that thought from- the idea that prayer connects those of us in the body of Christ. It was only afterwards that I read about that concept in our spiritual guide.

The same day that I made that promise to that special little girl, we got the opportunity to go to liturgy afterwards. I managed to write her name on a slip of paper and have it placed on the altar. I couldn't help but feel that that was what God wanted me to do in that moment.

I continue to pray for her and I believe that we will be reunited someday soon God willing, whether it's for another game of 'cheat', or for the Father's heavenly banquet.

The Voice of an Angel and a Heart Made to Love All

- Marissa Gendy -

I found myself on this mission trip hoping that through it, I would be able to feel God in my life in an entirely different way. There were many little moments on my trip that proved to me the intensity of God's love and compassion on His children. One being when I had mentioned in English to my partner that I was hungry. The next day, a little boy showed up with two sandwiches and a bag of chips for us. The boy did not speak English, nor did he understand it. His desire to bring me food was purely out of love and compassion for his teachers. Many instances such as this built a closeness to God's love that I previously had never experienced.

I met a girl my first day teaching named Helena*. Helena

is around 10 years old. Helena had a younger sister who was in my class as well, and she made it her priority to look after her sister and make sure she felt safe and comfortable. I learned very early on that Helena was different from the other children. While many of them thanked and hugged me when I told them "Bravo" and "Helw Awi," (very good) she would barely acknowledge the praise my partner and I gave her. Additionally, it became apparent that she was the smartest girl in the room. Although obvious to my partner and I, she humbly hid her intelligence. Instead, she would subtly lend a helping hand, or ask questions for the kids who didn't fully understand certain concepts. The fact that she herself was extremely shy never took away from her desire to help others. As the opportunity for communication grew, I learned that as strong as her brain was, her heart was stronger. As intelligent as she was, she never carried herself with pride that prevented her from letting others learn or letting others shine. She would instead proudly cheer for them from the sidelines. I grew to admire her: her resilience, her tenacity, her kindness, her bravery, and most importantly her Christ-like nature. Every conversation with her made me feel closer to God, as if I had established a direct line of communication with Him; one which He would answer right away.

My comprehension of Arabic is good, however I struggle to articulate my thoughts. Helena made our communication simple. She would speak and I would answer as best as I could. When I didn't understand her, she would go home, learn the words in English and come the next day to explain to me what she meant. When she didn't understand me, she would go to my partner and ask him to translate the words into English. Language was no barrier in our friendship. She showed me compassion and empathy when I struggled and did everything she could to make me feel comfortable, the same way she did for her sister.

One day in particular taught me a lesson I hope to never forget. My group-mates and I decided that on one of the Fridays, instead of having classes, we would combine all the classes and have a talent show. Many kids brought in their artwork, some sang beautiful hymns and songs and others put on elaborate productions. Every child that performed made me smile with incomparable joy. Helena had decided to perform a song with her little sister and some of her friends. As they began singing, I was amazed. Even amidst four girls, I could distinctly hear her voice. It was nothing like I had ever heard before. The subtle harmony she was able to sing rang throughout the church. I couldn't help but shut my eyes. I wanted her to continue singing for hours just so that I could hear her beautiful voice. Helena was a reserved and shy girl when it came to herself so this was the first time I saw her as just herself, independent of others. She had no obligation to another person, it was just her and the music. There was no pressure, obligation, regret or arrogance. It was just a girl singing a beautiful ode to her country. At the end of the song, each girl sang a solo and as I took in every sung word, I waited patiently for Helena's part. And then, there it was: the voice of an angel. No music, or dancing, or even other voices, just Helena's voice and the audience listening. At this point, I was unable to see because of the tears that had flooded my eyes. The little girl that had helped every person in the room, including me, was standing in front of me and finally doing something for herself.

After the performance was finished, I left the church to stand outside and catch my breath. She had left me speechless. I cried for ten minutes, mourning the words I would never be able to say because of our language barrier. Luckily, after those ten minutes of undeniable sadness, a local representative that I had been working with found me and asked me why I was so distraught. I was able to explain to her way I was so sad and what had happened. She looked at me and asked one simple question, "Why does this make you sad, and not filled with joy?" I didn't understand it then, but I believe I am starting to understand it as I continue to reflect on my trip. I was sad because I knew, before even having a conversation with Helena, that she wouldn't see what I had seen in her. I knew that when I spoke to her about the experience, she would see it as just a fun moment she got to share with her sister.

I walked back in at the end of the talent show and spoke to Helena about how amazed I was by her. As we spoke, she told me about how nervous she was to perform and how the only reason she did so was to stand beside her sister. I couldn't help but interject and tell her what I had witnessed. I told her about how her voice had put me into tears and how in all my life I had never heard real music until I heard her voice. I told her about how amazing her gift of singing was and how one day she could be the most famous singer in all of Egypt. Before I could continue speaking, she began to cry and said something along these lines: "I do not deserve praise like this. I am nothing without God. Say good job to God, not to me." That was the second time in less than an hour that Helena had made me cry.

Helena changed my life with those words. She showed me something I had forgotten as I got older and school, work, and my social life became more time-consuming and difficult. Helena showed me the beauty in thankfulness and in humility. Helena taught me that ultimate peace comes through strengthening my relationship with God. Not one time did she ask for anything in return when helping the other kids in my class. Not one time did she look for praise or validation in the good she did. Not one time did she forget to remind me that the good in her came from God and not from her own character. Not one time did I look at her and fail to see Christ. Her interactions with others around her taught me the real meaning of love, a love God intended. Helena taught me that love at its simplest form is unconditional. Despite flaws, mistakes, misstep, misdirection, or challenge, she loved her neighbor. She proved to me that it is possible for God to love me and any person despite the sins I have committed. Helena taught me that nothing good in life comes without God. He is the source of every blessing, gift, and wonderful moment. He paves the way for our success and happiness, and guides us through our trials and tribulations.

I sincerely wish for Helena and I to cross paths again. I am unsure of how our meeting affected Helena, but personally, I know that Helena is a little girl I will remember for the rest of my life. A girl with the voice of an angel and a heart made to love all. I pray she remains safe, healthy, and happy, inspiring every person that is privileged enough to know her.

*For the sake of privacy, the name of the individual in the story has been changed to Helena.

The Bracelet That I Will Always Cherish

- Ameer Zaki -

I was so fortunate to be accepted to serve on the first-ever Coptic Orphans trip, The 21, from June to July 2022. My fellows and I were based in the small town in Minya, Egypt. The trip was such a remarkable opportunity filled with blessings, and this is just one account of one of the blessings that I received while on this trip.

It was our final day in Minya. We planned a fun, cheerful and soaking wet party for the children that day. We found throughout our service, the kids loved playing with water. Water games were unanimously the games they enjoyed playing the most, and with accessible taps in the courtyard, they had a wide range of weapons at their disposal. Water guns, water balloons, water bottles, you name it. They proved how resourceful they were, limited only by their imagination and desire.

We made the reckless mistake one day of bringing the water guns to the school, thinking that the children would be patient and obedient enough to wait until we gave them permission to play with them. Once one child got their hands on a gun, it spun out of control. Before we knew it, multitudes were running around the courtyard (Coptic Orphans fellows included) shooting, throwing and squirting water. It was crazy but it was amazing. However, we learned our lesson that day, taking all the guns home and only bringing them in on a few allocated days.

On our final day of service, we came to class early to prepare for the party. We agreed that we would let them run wild on this day. Guns and water from minute one; it was going to be a mess, but what a time we would have. We came to the school, and the unimaginable happened: there was no water. Village water cuts were not uncommon, they happened several times during our stay. However, most times the water cut would last for a short amount of time and for a maximum of 2 hours. This time was different. Despite the setback, we were still determined to have a brilliant last-day party.

We had some other stations planned that day, but we still had to come up with more games. Fortunately, I was blessed to be serving alongside 7 brilliant fellows. We all put our heads together and figured it out. We would split the children into 4 groups and assign them to dance, balloon popping, dodgeball, and paper airplane stations. One of the fellows and I were assigned to run the dodgeball station. Finally, after all the preparation and hiccups, the day had begun. The sun was beaming down, the temperature was boiling (as usual) and the kids were running around. My co-fellow and I were carrying out our first dodgeball game. A little girl came up to me and gained my attention, temporarily shifting me from my dodgeball duties. She brought us to one side, knelt down and reached into her bag. She brought out a typical Coptic bracelet. The ones compiled of squares, strings, and beads, with pictures of God and the saints on different panels. She handed it to me, and truthfully, I don't remember the whole conversation, but I remember she told me (in Arabic) to wear it, and: "If you ever take it off, I will kill you!"

Over the previous three weeks, I had developed a connection with the students of my class. I learned all of their names (it might have helped that a fifth of my boys were named Karas) and grew closer to them. We would regularly play games with other classes, and the children were eager to meet and get to know us. Because of this, not only did I become familiar with the children that Christ gave me to teach, but also many of the other children. This girl however, was different. She was in none of my classes. I have no recollection of visiting her home, playing with her at school, or even talking with her. I did not know her name.

I was amazed that someone who I felt certain I hadn't interacted with, who I seemingly hadn't developed a relationship with, and who was experiencing economic poverty, went out of her way to give me a gift, and to give it with such passion. It was so loving, it was Christ-like, it was an example of His grace. The gift in isolation may have seemed like something that we, in the West, may see as common and not worthy of a second look, but it was so much more than that coming from the hands of a fatherless child. This child may very well have used all she had to buy myself and my peers a bracelet. It was one of the best material gifts (although it represents so much more than that) I have ever received. After receiving the gift I finally asked for her name which she said was Mary*. We then took a couple of photos together so I would always have a way to remember her.

I am writing this over 250 days after receiving her and God's blessings on that day. I have heeded her words and tried to do her will. I have not taken the bracelet off. Out of the 12 panels which each had their own pictures on them, all but 3 have peeled off. I think it is worth noting that those three happen to be The Lord Himself, Saint Bashnouna, and the iconic image of the Virgin Saint Mary with her son Jesus Christ. God works in mysterious ways, but I think it is clear why these ones have so far remained. One of the fellows whom I served with has since sponsored Mary, donating regularly to Coptic Orphans and supporting the charity and Mary. Coptic Orphans offers the ability for the sponsor and child to write letters to one another, which my co-fellow has used to write to her.

I was blessed enough to serve and be served whilst on

this trip. I received multiple gifts from children, fellows, and my incredible coordinator, Olivia. However, I chose to write about Mary due to the fact that I didn't even know this girl before that day, and the manner, joy and passion in which she showed me a fraction of God's love. To others this may seem like a simple story of a child giving a servant a gift. And simply, it is just that. However, to me, it was so much more.

*For the sake of privacy, the name of the individual in the story has been changed to Mary.

It Was A Surprise To All Of Us

- Anne Joseph -

Coptic Orphans' Valuable Girl Project pairs up Big Sisters in university with Little Sisters, whom they mentor and tutor while learning important life skills together. I met Demiana* on one of our first days just getting to know the girls in a class of Little Sisters. We started teaching them about family and how they could translate various words into English. My class partner and I started encouraging the girls to go and write a family member (father, mother, etc.) in English on the whiteboard. To our delight, many girls volunteered, but there was a shy little girl named Demiana sitting quietly and keeping to herself. I decided to go up to her and say "Come on darling, your turn."

Fast forward to our story; to make the game more fun, we blind folded the girls. My class partner and I blind folded all of the students, including Demiana. She stood at the whiteboard and wrote the word 'brother' on her own. We cheered for her and she sat back down. What happened next stunned me for the rest of the day. Her supervisor informed us that Demiana has a neurological condition. She cannot read, speak, or write properly. She hadn't written out a coherent word or even held a pen in a very long time. For her to write this word on the whiteboard while blindfolded was an amazing feat.

Demiana started out as a shy little girl, but by the end of our trip, she was standing with occupation flash cards teaching the girls how to pronounce various professions. I was honestly so grateful to have been a small part of God's plan for this little girl. I was personally struggling with finding a purpose for my life, however, by the end of the trip, and after taking the blessing of many other girls like Demiana, I knew that I was part of something much bigger than myself.

*For the sake of privacy, the name of the individual in the story has been changed to Demiana.

The Most Generous Love

- Marina Sawires -

In winter of 2023, I had the blessing of going to Egypt to serve with Coptic Orphans on their Serve to Learn trip. Myself and three other servants from across America and Australia were sent to a small village in Qena to teach English to children between the ages of 7 and 14. Quite frankly, this trip changed my life. We were going to Egypt to serve but we were truly the ones who were served through an outpouring of generosity, compassion, love and faith from the children and the local servants alike. This service was evident from the second that we arrived at our local accommodation in the village. As our microbus parked and we emptied our luggage from the trunk and the roof of the car, we found several young boys from around the neighborhood gathering around us and asking how they could lend a hand. Within minutes, each one of them had clung to a suitcase and made their way up several flights of stairs to drop our luggage off at the door of our apartment. We were strangers to these boys, they did not even know our names, but they were generously prepared to serve us without question. "And whatever you do, do it heartily, as to the Lord and not to men, knowing that from the Lord you will receive the reward of the inheritance; for you serve the Lord Christ." (Colossians 3:23-24) Each of the people that we met in Qena personified generous service as if they were serving The Lord Himself.

† † †

My group was split into pairs of servants, with each pair being responsible for one classroom. We taught two classes each day, and in the evenings we accompanied our Coptic Orphans local representative on their home visitations. Local representatives are individuals who are responsible for personally serving each of the kids who are enrolled in Coptic Orphans' Not Alone Program (NAP). NAP is a program that financially, academically and socially supports families who have lost the father figure in the home. My group decided that we were going to pray Matthew 5:1-16 (the Beatitudes) with each of the families during their visitation. Oddly enough, we quickly found this passage coming up time and time again throughout our time in the service. A few days after we had begun reading this passage on our home visitations, we attended a Liturgy where the Gospel reading was coincidentally the reading from the Beatitudes. One week later, we were visiting the home of a boy in NAP whose father abandoned the family and whose mother suffered severe mental delay as a result of a health-related accident. This delay left his mother almost nonverbal and with minimal mental and motor function. Prior to this incident, the mother was an active servant who loved to read the Bible and serve in the Sunday School. When we asked the boy's grandmother if she could hand us a Bible so that we could all read a passage together, she handed us the mother's personal Bible from underneath her pillow. We opened her Bible to find several icons and markings placed at chapter 5 of the book of Matthew, the Gospel that we would be reading with our student. As we began reading the passage out loud, we found the mother joining us and saying with us "Blessed are the poor in spirit for theirs is the Kingdom of Heaven, Blessed are those who mourn for they shall be comforted..." She slowly recited every verse of the Beatitudes with us. My visitation partner and I were stunned. This woman's condition was incredibly severe. She spends most of her days on her bed. Her mother takes care of her around the clock and her only child is being raised primarily by his grandmother and the rest of the mother's extended family. However, it was so clear to see that even in her condition, her heart was with Christ. We hear all the time of the mercies of God and how He never abandons any one of His sheep, but we were truly blessed to see His mercy exemplified in the strength of her faith. From the outside it seemed that God had taken so much from her, but He was so clearly present with her in the midst of all of her suffering. He really never left her side.

As the weeks progressed, we kept having conversations about the Beatitudes with our kids and their families. Each person's experience with this Gospel helped us grow. During our last week of service, we were walking home from one of our visitations and decided to step into a local Church to pray. We ran into one of our local representatives and began chatting with him. He was accompanied by two young deacons who were practicing the Liturgy Gospel reading that their deacons class was going to be tested on that weekend. We asked them if we could listen as they practiced with their servant. They were hesitant but they agreed, and then in Arabic they began reciting "And seeing the multitudes, He went up on a mountain..." My visitation partner and I were speechless. It was a true full circle moment for us to hear and meditate on this Gospel that The Lord time and time again kept bringing to our attention. My entire group felt incredibly thankful to God for giving us encouragement in such a visible way throughout our service.

† † †

During our class time several of the kids shared stories about their interactions with their siblings or their parents. During one of our classes, a student raised his hand to share a story of a miracle that had happened with him that was related to his father. This child is part of the NAP program, and his father passed away years ago. In Arabic he recounted a miraculous story that happened to him several years ago: "My father passed away due to a heart condition, and this heart condition was genetically passed on to me. My father had just passed away from the condition when the doctors discovered that I had the same condition as him. As we were on our way to the cardiologist to check on the condition of my heart, we stopped and visited Anba Kyrillos. He took a cross and tapped it on my chest three times and said to my mother: 'Go to the doctor and have him perform a check-up, you will find that your son has been healed.' So, we went to my doctor's appointment and he performed the check-up and we found out that I was totally healed." Of course, we were in absolute awe at this entire story. But I was personally in awe of the child himself and his demeanor in our classroom. He was only 10 years old, but he recounted the death of his father with a sense of peace and acceptance that you would not even expect of somebody who was well into their adult life. The trauma of watching your father pass away and then finding out that you inherited the very disease that took him from you is unimaginable. However, our student mentioned the suffering so briefly and immediately lit up as he was describing the way that God worked in his life through Anba Kyrillos. Seeing how pure his joy and faith were amid such an intense tribulation was a testament to myself, my co-teacher and all of his peers.

† † †

The way that the children conducted themselves always taught me a new lesson. During one early morning liturgy I saw one of my students sitting on the men's side of the church and not dressed as a deacon as he was accustomed. I went up to him and told him to go have Abouna bless his tonya (deacon garment) and serve in the altar. He firmly shook his head no. When I asked him why he refused to serve as a deacon that day, he told me he couldn't tell me. He looked visibly upset that he was missing out on the blessing of the service. His servant quickly came and encouraged him and told him to come serve in the altar. After much hesitation he smiled and agreed to serve in the altar like he was used to. This young child felt in his heart that he was not fit to serve in the altar that day, for reasons that he kept between him and Christ. However, his servant came and reminded him of how merciful and graceful our Lord is. This young boy embodied true humility while his servant embodied true compassion.

☦ ☦ ☦

One thing that became apparent in our class was how eager the kids were to learn. We focused our time on teaching English by way of spiritual concepts as well as lessons about health, and life skills. Day by day our class grew. Kids from the village and from nearby villages who were not on our roster joined our class eager to learn this new material. When they heard that we were teaching this material, they went and bought new notebooks and pencils just so they could learn the vocabulary and spiritual concepts that we were teaching. We taught 'Our Father' in English as a warm-up throughout the course

The Most Generous Love

of the three weeks, adding a line or two each day. One day as we were still working through learning the full prayer, I had a student come up to me with his pen and notebook begging me to please write down the entire prayer in both English and Arabic. He wanted to learn the entire prayer and have it in a place where he could access it when he went home. This excitement to learn and grow was consistent in the rest of the students. We taught a verse of the day that aligned with our curriculum each class period. On one of the days, we were short on time and did not get a chance to teach this verse. The next day several students came up to us and made it clear to us that they were very upset that our class went a day without learning a new verse. The students would stay after class ended to recite the verse of the day that they had memorized, as well as several other verses that they went home and learned independently the day prior. They were hungry to learn about the Bible and to take what they learned and use it in their daily lives. Lessons about love, forgiveness and service were quickly implemented in their actions towards one another. Rather than get upset with their friend if they said something that hurt their feelings as they often did throughout week one, by week three they'd turn and respond with "may God forgive you," and continue jotting down their verses. They were so receptive to the word of God and to letting it truly work in them.

† † †

Our NAP students came from villages that are located all over the Qena governorate. On one of our home visitations, we went to visit one of the further villages where our students lived. We drove an hour from the village that we were staying in, then we took a tok tok into the center of the village and walked the rest of the way to the home that we would be visiting. By the time we reached the last home that we would be visiting, my visitation partner and I were exhausted from the commute. As we joked about how tired we were, our local representative reminded us that the kids made this journey every single day just to participate in the program. In the midst of their mid-year break they happily woke up at 6 am to leave the house by 7 and get on a microbus that then picked up the rest of the kids from the village and brought them to the church. The journey took an hour and a half going and an hour and a half returning. They spent 3 hours a day just commuting to come to class, and they rarely missed a day. When they got to class, they did not grumble or complain. They were excited to see us, see each other and learn what we would be teaching that day. Every day, the kids would go down to the church cantine and buy snacks with their allowance money. Every single day without fail each of them would offer us handfuls of chips, endomi (Egyptian ramen) and sweets that they bought. If we thanked them for their kind offer and refused to accept their food, they were visibly upset and repeatedly kept offering their snacks until we accepted and ate with them. The kids would go so far as to go downstairs and purchase three of the same snack. One for themselves, one for myself and one for my partner. They are truly the most generous people I have ever met. We witnessed the same sentiment in so many of the homes that we visited. Mothers would put out their own family's eid sweets for us to eat and share in. On our way out, they would beg us to stay and have dinner with them. It was so clear to see that contentment and generosity are their way of life. These qualities are traits that the kids see personified in their families every single day, and because of this, they so naturally flowed into all of the children's own actions.

† † †

The people that I met in Qena are the most generous, compassionate and Christ-like individuals I have ever met. I will forever be grateful to them for so graciously offering us the warmest welcome into their homes and families. I deeply admire each of them and I am so thankful to have had the blessing of spending time with them, laughing with them and learning from them through Serve To Learn.

A Faith Truly Unshaken

- Youanaa Gendy -

As part of our daily schedule on the Coptic Orphans' The 21 service trip, we visited many students in their homes. We would try to get to know them more and learn about their personal lives as well as their mothers' lives. We would learn a lot about the kids' relationships with their mothers, their family history, hobbies, and roles at home. Each one of these kids had great attributes and characteristics to offer. However, a young boy named Tadros* stood out to me for numerous reasons.

Before talking about the visitation, I'll talk about Tadros's personality in the classroom. From the first day of class, it was clear to see that Tadros was a good kid. He was always willing to help, listen, join the conversation, and behave. Whenever we asked everyone to be quiet, he was the first to listen. No matter who spoke to him or tried to distract him, Tadros was always following the rules. He knew right from wrong. He was able to resist the distractions and focus on what he was supposed to be doing. This was also reflected in his ability to withstand tribulations and never lose faith, which I will discuss further later on. Overall, Tadros was the embodiment of a perfect student. He later revealed to us that he was also the embodiment of God's word.

When it came time for us to visit Tadros in his home, I was very excited. I had seen how great of a kid he was in class and was curious about what his environment was like at home and how it shaped him into who he is today. As soon as we knocked on the door we were greeted by the stereotypical yet amazingly warm Egyptian hospitality. I immediately felt welcomed and loved; something both Tadros and his mother put forward. I quickly realized that the positive space that Tadros's mom created for him had a great deal to do with who Tadros was. He could not be loving or kind if he had not been repeatedly exposed to love and kindness by his mother and in his home. It was the foundation that he grew up on and spent most of his time practicing. This showed me how important it is for us to have a solid foundation for our faith. It made me realize how important our time is and how investing it in the right things can determine our core values.

First, I want to focus on Tadros's mom and her strong faith. Tadros's mother is named Martina*. Understanding Martina's circumstances are crucial to fully comprehending how strong her faith and love for God are. Similar to many traditional Egyptian families, Martina's husband had been the primary source of income in their household. Unfortunately, he drowned and passed away suddenly a few years before our visit. This left Martina to take care of their only child. Such a loss is not something you can overcome easily. It is something that most people never fully recover from. However, Martina stood strong for her son. From the moment Martina became a widow, she strived to give Tadros the best and most fruitful life she could. When we were at their house, Tadros mentioned the number of monasteries and churches he had visited and how often he goes. I was shocked by this since most of the monasteries he mentioned were quite far from where he lived. They were hours away and they did not have a car, but his mother always found a way. Martina told us that by exposing her son to God's most sacred places, she hopes he feels and experiences the grace and love of God. Throughout all of Martina's tribulations, pain, and suffering, she never neglected her son. But how? Martina went through some of the most painful experiences anyone can go through, yet still managed to fill Tadros's life with love and hope.

"Have I not commanded you? Be strong and of good courage; do not be afraid, nor be dismayed, for the LORD your God is with you wherever you go." (Joshua 1:9). Martina was a perfect representation of this verse. Because of her unconditional and endless love for Tadros, her determination to give him a fruitful life, and her courage, wisdom, and her strength; I saw the word of God reflected in her actions, aspirations, and efforts. Just like God protects, guides, and loves us, Martina did the same for Tadros.

Ultimately, Tadros was able to see the great lengths his mother went to make his life wonderful. His mother pushed him to pursue God in every way. Tadros told us, "My mom does not deprive me of anything." At this point in the visitation, I started tearing up. The amount of love Tadros had for his mother blew me away. Tadros showed great appreciation, understanding, and empathy for his mother. That made me think... how is a child this young able to have such a selfless, loving, and understanding heart? How is he able to have such strong faith when his life has been flipped upside down? How is he able to overcome his grief, and support his mother as she supports him? All these questions lingered in my mind throughout the whole visitation.

As time went on, we were making small talk and asking questions about Tadros's life. To my surprise, he was part of a wide variety of activities. Aside from Church activities, Tadros coded, did taekwondo, and visited many sacred places. You could tell Tadros was ambitious and curious. At one point in the visitation, Tadros was eagerly asking his mom to show us a video because he was so proud of himself. Martina pulled out her phone and was showing us a video of Tadros going down a water slide. What made this video extra special was Tadros's fearlessness. Since Tadros's dad had drowned, it created a mental block between Tadros and swimming or anything related to water. That invoked another question. How was Tadros able to overcome such a deep-rooted fear? Tadros showed us how freeing God is. He showed us what it means to "Trust in the Lord with all your heart and lean not on your own understanding" (Proverbs 3:5). Tadros put his fears, worries, and mental restrictions onto God and fully trusted him. He knew God would take care of him going down that water slide. Even when given every reason to not trust that water slide or the swimming pool, Tadros chose to put his trust in God rather than in his circumstances.

Every single question I mentioned earlier boiled down to one answer. God. Martina's strength and love for Tadros came from God. Tadros's fearlessness and love for his mother came from God. Everything Martina and Tadros stood for was a direct embodiment of what God tells us—his children—to be. Like most, I often get caught up in my misfortunes and use them as excuses to lose faith. However, after meeting Tadros and Martina, I realized that God never leaves us short of anything. Through all the tribulations life has to offer, God gives us everything we need to get through it and grow. If someone like Martina can stand strong in her faith after how agonizing her life has been, why can't I? I am grateful to have had the opportunity to meet such God-loving and God-fearing people who have been, and continue to be, an inspiration to me.

*For the sake of privacy, the names of the individuals

in the story have been changed to Tadros and Martina, appearing throughout the stories in this order.

The Day God Hugged Me

- Marena Soliman -

"Assuredly, I say to you, unless you are converted and become as little children, you will by no means enter the kingdom of heaven. Therefore whoever humbles himself as this little child is the greatest in the kingdom of heaven. Whoever receives one little child like this in My name receives Me" (Matthew 18:3-5).

I've never really had a travel bug. I've never been enticed by the idea of getting on a plane and travelling in excess of 24 hours. However, there was one thing I knew; for some reason, God wanted me on this trip. I still remember when Abouna was asking who wanted to go. I quickly raised my hand without giving it much thought. When I told my family and friends that I would be travelling to Egypt; they laughed, knowing that I was very much against visiting the motherland. Despite the stories and warnings that were brought to my attention, a certain fire still seemed to burn inside of me. I didn't know what it was, but I knew that I had to go. The weeks leading up to the trip were filled with feelings of anxiety, stress and even regret. Let's face it, there was only one thing I could do; pray. Pray that I had made the right decision and that everything would be okay.

† † †

Egypt. It was the start of Service week. I didn't know what to expect. I've had minimal exposure to people who are unfortunate, sick, elderly or afflicted with some form of disability. Walking down the streets of Egypt led me to a realization of how blind I had been back home in Sydney. It became clear that God wanted to alter my perspective on life. I finally understood how the blind man felt when the Lord created eyes for him to see. What I had seen was something I could never easily explain. The whirlwind of emotions I had experienced meant that something was changing within me. I missed my family, my friends and my life. All I remember was walking in and out of service, taking breathing breaks, as I was very much overwhelmed by the situation I was in. I "feel" too much, perhaps more than the average human. Because of this, I knew I would continue to linger in this state for the days to come.

Halfway through the week, we went to a house filled with children who had various disabilities. At this point, I was an emotional wreck, even more so than at the beginning of the week. I felt vulnerable, insecure and weak. I was a bit concerned that I wouldn't be able to handle the situation that we were walking into. I walked in not knowing what to do, whom to speak to, or how to speak with them as my Arabic skills are pretty much non-existent. I was really lost. Most of the children couldn't communicate via words anyway, so maybe this worked to my advantage. I was hesitant and cautious. Whilst slowly walking around, awkwardly greeting everyone, there was a young boy who caught my attention. Shenouda*. When the disciples tried to keep the children away from the Lord while He was teaching the multitude, the Lord stood and said, "bring the little children to Me". He knew their innocence. He knew their purity, and He was about to reveal that to me in the simplest way. The first thing Shenouda did was hug me! It caught me by surprise, causing me to flinch in my delicate state. I was shocked, yet immediately filled with overwhelming peace. Time froze as if the world stood still on its axis. It was like nothing around me mattered anymore. Every ounce of anxiety, fear and awkwardness had diminished.

Shenouda's hug felt like home. It was at this moment that I could truly understand the meaning of unconditional love. Although it was something so familiar to me, it was also something I was too scared to willingly give or even display. Filled with such love, I wondered, was this how the prodigal son felt when his father embraced him upon his return? There, in that exact moment, is where I felt my Father's embrace. I realized that Shenouda's hug was a hug from God. Only He knew that this was the only way to give me comfort.

Anyone who knows me, knows that I value hugs. Hugs are just not something I take for granted and I certainly do not give them away freely. For some, they act as a simple greeting, but to me, they are so much more. They are the epitome of true love. There was something special about this hug. Something special about Shenouda. With one hundred percent certainty I could say that this hug was a timely gift from God. He knew how much I needed this hug. It was so simple, and yet such a pure act of love. A hug from a child — no pretense, no hidden motives. I could barely fight back the tears of joy as I contemplated His loving touch in my time of need. I quickly realized that God had just answered my prayer in the most tangible and personal way. I went to Egypt thinking that I would be serving the unfortunate, but in reality, it was I who was being served. I was the one who needed service. I had nothing to offer them. Nothing whatsoever. All I could do was learn from those around me. The young, the old, the sick and the needy. For the next couple of weeks, I was in awe of everything around me and fell in love with every aspect of Egypt. All because of a hug! Something we take for granted daily. Who knew? What I would do to be hugged like that again... to be hugged by God.

We are currently living in a world where everything is uncertain, and the fear of the unknown is driving us to do unspeakable things to each other. What we don't realize is that people have been living in these conditions their entire lives, but their approach is completely different to ours. These beautiful human beings, like Shenouda, are an embodiment of God's love and mercy! They are a true reflection of the beatitude which states, "Blessed are the pure in heart for they shall see God" (Matthew 5:8).

They have every reason to worry and stress, yet they don't. They instead are filled with such a stillness because they know that He is taking care of them. That hug from Shenouda was my reminder. It was a reminder to be still. It was a reminder that my God is bigger than all my worries and anxieties. It was a reminder that God would protect me and deliver me from every uncertainty as He did with Moses and the Israelites. It was my reminder that truly, God is Love.

*For the sake of privacy, the name of the individual in the story has been changed to Shenouda.

Encountering Christ

- Marina Fahim -

It was our first day arriving at our site, and my partners and I were settling into our accommodation, where we were supposed to stay for the next three weeks. Our local coordinator Vivian* told us that she would go buy bread for us, so my friend Alice* and I decided to go with her. Vivian was locking the door when I noticed an old woman living in the home next door. She was looking out of her door while standing behind her doorstep. It was giving me the impression that she was waiting for someone to arrive. She turned her head and we made eye contact, so she smiled at me with her warm smile and I smiled back. Then she asked me "Heya el sa3a kam delwa2ty ya habebty ?" which means what time is it now sweetheart? I told her that it was 9 pm. An hour later, after we bought the bread and we were on our way home, I found this old kind lady in the same position again. Lost or curious maybe? As we were approaching, another person was walking near her. She asked that person the same question that she asked me, and they answered her. The whole situation seemed strange to me. I mean, why go outside your house to ask about the time? I decided to ask my local coordinator about her, and it was then that she told me that this old lady doesn't own a clock. To learn the time, she goes out of her home to ask whoever is passing by to tell her the time. At that moment, I cannot describe the feeling that overcame me. It was a feeling of empathy mixed with privilege. Tears filled my eyes instantly and without thinking I found myself asking my coordinator if we could go to buy a clock and give it to her. Vivian told me "Heya msh bt3rf te2ra" which means she can't read, so there is no point in buying the clock. I thought to myself, will she live dependent for so long? Will she go out of her house hoping for anyone to pass, to ask them about the time? These questions filled my mind, while I instantly became aware of the feeling of 'taking things for granted.' I never thought that someone could live without owning a clock while I simultaneously strive to make sure that I have an Apple Watch Series 8 (the newest version at the moment). This was my first encounter in this village. I understood that Christ sent me here to introduce me to this simple life. It felt like a wake-up call, seeing these people trusting in their God, that He will provide for them.

† † †

During the second week, my group of three other servants and I were awake late into the night to prepare for the next day's lesson and activities. One of us decided to boil some water to make some tea. Oh yes, we had developed a new addiction during this period. I've learned that offering tea is the best gift you can possibly present in upper Egypt. Anyway, while she went into the kitchen, I received a message on my phone from my manager back home. It was a very weird and unexpected message. My manager notified me that I was fired from my job since I had been overseas for an extended period of time. Despite the request form that I filled out with the exact dates of my trip, they found reason to fire me. To be honest, at first, I felt annoyed and speechless. I was completely distracted that night. The next morning, I woke up and I decided to share this news with the rest of the group. So I started with "Good morning girls, I just got fired!" A minute of silence filled the room, however, that silence was broken when another member of my group replied, " Oh my gosh, I also got fired from my job this morning. I don't know why, I told them that I would be away and they seemed okay with it." Alice tried to comfort both of us by using sweet, kind sentences, and a pat on the shoulder. Two hours later, Alice came up to me and told me that her master's application isn't going through for some reason. She was having such a difficult day and it ended up really distracting her during class. The following day, Monica*, the fourth member of our group, was walking down the stairs and suddenly twisted her ankle badly, which made it impossible for her to leave our apartment for two days. Because of this, she also missed the service. We did not understand what was happening. Why were all of these unexplainable events happening to us? When we returned to our home, we all realized how distracted we were due to all of the events in our lives. We understood how this could be a trick from the devil to distract us from serving our girls. At that moment we decided to leave everything behind, reminding ourselves that we were there for Him and for His daughters. I was always a big fan of how Abba Anthony the Great overcame the attacks of the devil in the desert through prayer. It never crossed my mind that we could experience a form of warfare other than the invisible kind, even though we are not monastics. It is not like I left my water pot and followed Him like St. Photini (John 4:28); it was a figuratively small sacrifice but allowed us to taste what it is like to follow Him (Matthew 16:24).

† † †

One day in between our two class sessions, Alice and I were standing on a beautiful narrow street with crosses engraved on the walls and the doors, right beside our classroom, when I realized that a young boy was looking out the window mischievously (pretending to be invisible). This scene drew a smile to my face, so I told Alice to look at how curious he is, and she laughed as well. I then decided to call him down to come to us. I started the conversation by asking about his name, and he replied Mina*. So I asked Mina to come down and play with us. At first, he refused to come to meet with us, however, as soon as I mentioned that we had stickers, he was standing by our side within seconds. His eyes were filled with great joy when we handed him the stickers sheets, as if we offered him an expensive gift. A couple of days later, I noticed that Mina was coming to meet us every day during our break, just to say hello. His commitment to just seeing us was precious and endearing to my heart. During the last week of our mission, Mina came to me accompanied by a couple of his friends, asking for more stickers, saying "Only for them, not for me, I have enough". It occurred to me how grateful Mina is. Then he approached me, hugged me and said I'll be going to Deer el Malak (the monastery of the Archangel Michael in Naqada) with my father. We will be staying for a couple of nights, so I will not see you when I come back, but I will pray for you! This sentence may just seem outwardly lovely but its effect on me was much deeper. The fact that he shared that he will remember me in his prayers, and the fact that he assured me that he is praying for me, was life-changing. I pray that Mina will always have this loving and unceasingly praying heart.

† † †

This is one of the stories that really touched my heart. On the third day of Jonah's fast, we all decided to attend liturgy in one of the ancient monasteries that was not occupied by monks and was only used as a church for the congregation. The monastery of St. Victor Son of Romanus in Hijâza. After we had an Agape meal with the priest of this church, they informed us that Hijâza (the name of the village) is known for its trade in wood carving and carpentry. For this reason, our local coordinator planned for us to visit the main wood factory. Here, the process, from finding the trunk of the tree to polishing the products with olive oil, happens. During our visit, our tour guide showed us a huge machine that cuts any type of thick trunk into small pieces. I was personally impressed by how developed this factory was, even though it was located in a small village. While wandering around the enormous machine, I noticed a black and white picture of an old man who had a long and grey beard. I thought to myself, why do they have this man's picture on the machine. I vocalized this question to the person who was showing us around. He started his response by first taking a deep breath, which to me seemed like a moment of remembrance. Then he looked at me and replied: "This is our beloved Boutros, actually his name is Pierre". I was intrigued by his first sentence, so I asked him to tell me more about Pierre, and why they call him Boutros and not Pierre. He replied: " Telling his story to people is my favorite thing to do. Pierre was a French catholic friar who decided to come here not to help the poor by providing them with food, but by teaching them a trade that will provide them with a job and source of income. Pierre is from a high-class family in Paris. He decided one day to leave everything to join the fraternity. He chose poverty and simplicity. Then, his order decided to send him and another friar named François to Hijâza, which at the time was an uneducated and poor community, where many were unemployed and struggling financially. When the two friars arrived here, they did not go around to preach, they instead showed us love and compassion. They would help us with our French homework, even though they didn't speak Arabic. We thought to ourselves, how will they survive? They do not speak our language. But showing Christ's love did not require a specific language." I was astonished by such a story that highlighted the true meaning of a consecrated life to Christ. I asked him why Pierre wore a "galabeya" (the Egyptian tunic) and not his habit. He answered: "I myself asked him the same question and Pierre replied: "when Christ was incarnate and walked around Galilee, Nazareth and everywhere else in His ministry, He wore what they were wearing and ate what they were eating. He became man. And you do not want me to wear a galabeya? It is also very comfortable." That assured me that Christ sent us a great gift, which was Pierre. The simple people of the village called him Boutros (the Arabic version of Pierre or Peter). We are so grateful to this present moment, that we were taught this trade (carpentry/wood carving) from the hands of François and Pierre. They did not provide us with food, for they themselves were poor, but they gave us more than that. They provided us with education, independence, and a job. And they taught us how to acquire a relationship with Christ." I later asked our local coordinator if we could visit this house in the village and she agreed. It was a precious moment when I walked into their home and saw their simple chapel which had nothing but painted icons on the walls and some candles. I later discovered that they were the ones who painted them. I learned a great lesson through listening to their stories. They didn't hesitate to go to a completely different country with a culture and language foreign to them. They were complete strangers who were not equipped to stay in a small poor village in upper Egypt. But truly it was a declaration that Christ does not choose the qualified, but qualifies the chosen.

† † †

On one of our home visitations, we visited a family who was known for making items of furniture out of palm fronds/leaves. In Arabic this is called jarid alnakhl. My partner, Veronica,* and I were together for this home visit. We walked down a very narrow street leading to the home that we would be visiting. The neighborhood was distinctly simple and lacking some of the elements expected of a neighborhood. However, once we entered the house of Uncle Youssef*, we found him sitting on the ground cutting the palm fronds, using both his hands to cut and his feet to grasp and stabilize them. Twenty minutes into our visit, amid our conversation and laughs about how Veronica was attempting to cut the fronds; a poor old lady walked into the home to ask for alms. I did not expect anyone in that room to react to her request. Unexpectedly, Uncle Youssef got up and ran towards this old lady, gave her a pat on the shoulder and took her outside the home. He then gave her what he had in his pockets secretly. This may not seem like a very surprising interaction, but sitting in this small room, and being aware of the condition of this family, increased the implausibility of what occurred during this visit. I could only think in this moment of the fact that this man does not come from a highly affluent background. However, he possessed a high level of mercy and compassion towards others, even if it meant potentially not eating dinner that night. This small act of love and mercy that was presented by a simple man, who himself will likely forget the entire event, will forever live in my heart. The trust he had in Christ was exemplified and seen through his actions. Another man in his shoes could have claimed that he himself was poor and had little to give, and no one would be able argue with this reality. But for Uncle Youssef, being merciful and sharing the little he had was what made him different, and Christ-like.

*For the sake of privacy, the names of the individuals in the story have been changed to Vivian, Alice, Monica, Mina, Veronica and Uncle Youssef, appearing throughout the stories in this order.

A Life Changing Experience

- Anonymous -

Coptic Orphans is a charity that educates and nurtures fatherless children in more poverty-stricken parts of Egypt. Each child is registered in a program called 'Not Alone' in which they are assigned a volunteer representative who visits them biweekly and provides for the family's needs whether they be financial, emotional, or educational. Coptic Orphans also conducts another program called 'Serve To Learn.' This program gives servants from around the world the chance to come and serve these children in Egypt. This program consists of classes every morning and afternoon where the fellows teach the children lessons on the English language, hygiene habits and general spiritual principals. This is followed by home visitations every evening which are conducted alongside the volunteer reps who are assigned to each child. By the end of the three-week program, the fellows would have visited the homes of all the Not Alone children whom they have in their morning and afternoon classes.

Upon my arrival in Upper Egypt, I was taken aback by the level of gratitude and simplicity displayed by those around me. These two themes were echoed throughout more than one of my trips with Coptic Orphans. The simplicity of the locals extended beyond their modest clothing and housing conditions, it was visible in the way they smiled and the way they prayed, but mostly in the way they described their experiences with miracles and apparitions.

† † †

During one home visitation, we visited the house of an 11 year old boy named Karas,* who had a younger sister who was too young to attend our morning classes at the time. We spoke with their mother, and as the conversation developed, she decided to openly speak to us about a miracle she experienced around the time of her husband's death. When this woman was nearing the end of her pregnancy with her daughter, her husband sadly passed away. Her grief over her husband resulted in the newborn falling ill, and being sent to intensive care after birth. She sought the intercession of St. Mary and Abouna Faltaous, and prayed fervently saying, "Lord you have taken my husband, please don't take my daughter also." On a certain evening during these events, Karas' grandmother was home alone and spotted an icon of St. Mary shedding oil from the eyes. When she saw this, her instinct was to take the oil and anoint herself. When the mother returned to the home, the grandmother showed her the oil markings that were produced on the icon (at this point in the retelling of the story, the mother took out the icon and let me hold it to witness the oil marks at the eyes of St. Mary). Later on in the week, young Karas came up to his mother and told her "I had dream where an Abouna with a white beard took me on his back and flew around in amusement. He then gave me a bar of Molto (an Egyptian chocolate snack) and he told me to tell you not to worry about my sister, she will be just fine." After showing young Karas images of various saints, he picked out a picture of Abouna Faltaous and said, "that's the priest that came to me in my dream!" When we heard this story, we were all in awe and disbelief, and when the mother saw the look on our faces, she asked Karas to tell us about "the other time that he had a dream about Abouna Faltaous." To this Karas casually responded "oh yea, he came to me again but this time he brought me ice cream." The thing that made this encounter so special wasn't the beauty of the miracles or the blessings of this family, but it was the simplicity of the family's faith that was displayed in recounting the miracles so casually, as if these events happen regularly in day-to-day life. As my time in Egypt went on, I heard more and more miracles, and my faith was likewise strengthened.

† † †

My next encounter was at a house where the father had also passed away, however, this time the mother had gotten remarried and moved out to live with her husband. She left her two sons to the care of their grandparents to start a new life of her own. The condition of this home was extremely humble, as the income of the grandparents was close to nothing, and they were primarily supported by Coptic Orphans. In an attempt to share a word of comfort with this family, I shared with the boys and their grandparents how it takes me around 20 minutes of driving to get to church, and they are so blessed to get to walk to their nearest church to have communion. The grandfather hurried to express in a very passionate tone, "God is spoiling us with His blessings! We are living on holy land; we don't deserve to walk on the same dust that Christ himself walked on!" he then proceeded to direct his words at me and the servant beside me and said, "Christ came and visited us today when you entered our home, I thank you so much for acknowledging us in our poverty and visiting our home." At that point, I was speechless. For this man, our simple visit was like Christ himself had entered his home. All I could say was "we are the ones who received all the blessings, please keep us in your prayers." The visit proceeded as normal as the boys ran and brought their cymbals and sung a hymn for us. Afterwards, we read the Bible together and it was time to go home. At the end of the visit, we took a photo together and said our goodbyes. The grandpa once again exclaimed, "Christ entered my home today, thank you God, thank you God" as we shook hands in farewell, he bent over and tried to kiss my hand, I quickly pulled away and once again ... I was shocked and speechless, I didn't know how to respond, I pleaded with him to keep us all in his prayers. I knew the memory of visit would stick with me for a long time. This man really saw the image of Christ inside all the servants who walked into his house, it made me wonder how anyone can attain such levels of spirituality? "Blessed are the pure in heart for they shall see God" (Matthew 5:8), they shall see God in everything and in everyone. It was the purity of his heart! After walking out of this house, the word that occupied my mind was gratitude, I thought of all the times when people back home would rush to get the latest mobile or how distressed one would get when a bit of dirt lands on their new white shoes, and I compared that to the man who was grateful for the dust that he walks on.

† † †

One morning, I woke up to attend an early liturgy before our classes began for the day. It was about a 5 minute walk to get from our apartment to church, the streets were dark and empty so I tried not to make any noise so as to not wake up the locals. As I closed the apartment door behind me, I heard street dogs barking at a distance, but I couldn't see any. I cautiously made my way onto the street fearful of being spotted by a street dog. About five seconds into my walk, I saw 3 street dogs sprinting at me in the dark. I tried to remain calm and not appear as a threat, while I repeated the words 'Besm el Salib' (Arabic for "in the name of the

Cross") under my breath. As the dogs got closer, my methods of staying calm were not working, so I thought I'd make a run for it and just sprint my way to church. I quickly realized, that was not a good idea because they continued to chase me. As their barks echoed throughout the streets, they quickly caught up to about a meter behind me. At this point I didn't care about the locals and their sleep, I was shouting Besm el Salib so loudly hoping the dogs would get scared, but they did not get scared. When I felt their teeth on my ankles, I had to try other methods of calling for God's help, so I decided to turn around and sign them with the cross. When I did that, they instantly stopped barking and started running away and whining like they were scared of me. When I arrived at church, I was the most wide awake I have ever been for a 6 a.m. liturgy.

† † †

The following miracle was shared on a home visit where another servant was visiting a house. They later shared this story with us. The miracle proceeds as follows: There was a widow with four kids, and she explained that one time she had continuous bleeding for a prolonged period of time, and she was in much pain below her stomach. It didn't go away for months, so she sought medical help from her local doctor, who told her she had uterine cancer. She was not happy with this diagnosis and decided to go to Cairo for further testing. When she made the trip down to the city, she was again told that she had uterine cancer and needed surgery that would cost her 20,000 pounds, which was an impossible amount to acquire in her current financial state. The surgeon advised her to gather money from her friends, relatives and even the church, as her life depended on this surgery. The woman however refused to accept money from anyone and kept saying, "God gave me four children and took my husband and now He gave me this cancer, it's now up to Him to deal with the situation." She had faith that Christ would either heal her or find a way to take care of her children if she passed away. When she returned to her village, she said that she spent the whole night in prayer as she was unable to sleep. She groaned fervently seeking the intersession of St. Mary and saying to her, "you're a mother like me, you feel my pain. You know that my kids will have no one to care for them or make sure they are fed if I pass away." She continued to pray in this manner until she prayed herself to sleep. All of a sudden, she found herself in a white hospital room with a beautiful nurse standing by her bedside and looking down at her. Behind the nurse, near the door of the room, there stood a beautiful Doctor also with a gentle look on His face. The nurse then put her hand near the lady's lower stomach and lifted away holding something in her hand, as explained by the lady: "I saw my uterus in her hand". The nurse then proceeded to clean and wipe off any dirt that was on the uterus before placing it back into the lady's body and gently taping over her lower stomach to seal the surgery. It was obvious at this point that the beautiful nurse was St. Mary. As she turned to the Doctor and asked Him if He was happy with the surgery, the Doctor replied saying, "did you close up properly from here?" He pointed at the woman's stomach and in that instant the woman spotted nail holes in His wrists, and recognized that the Doctor was Jesus Himself supervising the surgery. St Mary then turned to her, gave her a pat on the shoulder and the woman woke up in her bedroom. When she went to her physicians and got her tests repeated, they came back negative of any signs of cancer.

† † †

This story was shared with me by another servant: They visited a house of a young boy who really loved soccer. As usual, they hung out and played a few card games, they also left a soccer ball as a gift for the boy but forgot to mention that this was a gift and he could keep it. As the servants made their way out of the house, the child came out running with the soccer ball yelling "you forgot your ball!" when the servants returned and explained to him that it was his to keep, the boy's eyes lit up and he looked at the ball like it was made of gold, he was in disbelief that it was his to keep. This once again highlights the simplicity of these children.

† † †

On my last day of service after 3 weeks of seeing these kids daily, it was time to say goodbye. When we were farewelling the kids in our class, many children and servants were brought to tears. The bond we formed

A Life Changing Experience

with the children was strong. Before we left, a 14 year old girl, Youanna*, came up to me and said "Ya Mister! Last night I was really upset because I knew that today was your last day and, in my sorrow I wrote you a poem, can I read it for you?" I responded, sure! For some context, this girl had never written any poems in her life and she greatly lacked in confidence when we first started the program. She lost her father, and upon his death, her mother abandoned their family. Youanna helps her older sister, who is engaged and about to be married, with caring for their two younger brothers, one of whom has a physical and mental disability.

The poem went as follows:

- I was a young child deprived of my father's embrace; I was all alone as I journeyed through the obstacles of life.

I was blown away by the quality of Arabic expressions that were used, they were extremely descriptive and elegant for someone her age to be using, the poem continued...

- I complained and I felt that I was alone in complete darkness I did not know my way because I was young.

She began to tear up as she said the following...

- But suddenly in the midst of my darkness, there was a beam of light and it illuminated my way.

- It assured me that I am not alone, but I have God and many people who love me alongside me,

By this point, tears were flowing from her eyes

- You were this light! You came to us with joy and happiness

- For this reason, I wanted to thank you and tell you that I am happy with this quenching light.

كنت طفلًا محرومًا من حضن ابي كنت لوحدي في درب حياتي و اشتكي و كنت اشعر اني وحيد في ظلامًا دامس لم اكن اعرف طريقي لانني كنت صغيرًا و لكن فجاة في وسط ظلامي التمست ضوءً و انار لي طريقي و عرفني اني لست وحدي بل من الله و معي اناسا كثيرون يحبونني و كان هذا الضوء انتم جئتم الينا و معكم فرحا و سعاده لذي احببت ان اشكركم و اقول لكم انا سعيده بهذا الضوء المشبع

This simple yet powerful message really stuck with me at the end of my trip, I felt that God was giving me a small taste how much He can accomplish through the most incompetent of servants.

*For the sake of privacy, the names of the individuals in the story have been changed to Karas and Youanna, appearing throughout the stories in this order.

The Healing Crosses

- Anonymous -

The following is an account of a miracle that I witnessed Saint George perform for a simple woman who loved him very much. I initially did not want to visit this monastery, but when I expressed this I was told that all the Monasteries in Egypt were incredibly special and all were built and survived on miracles after miracles. I wondered if this was true and if I would get to witness anything of the sort. Well, it's safe to say I got to witness something very special at St George Monastery.

† † †

When we arrived at St George Monastery, we noticed a small church that we wanted to go enter and pray in. When we entered the church, we could immediately hear an usual sound, which we quickly realized was the sound of people crying. It was a fairly small church and upon a close look, we realized that the sounds were coming from 2 women kneeling down at the curtain of the altar. It had a picture of St George on it. It instantly brought a feeling of discomfort. My first thought was that something had gone wrong and the women were crying and praying for a miracle. I quickly thought to pray an 'arrow prayer' and hope that everything was ok with them. They eventually left the church (still crying) and my family and I remained in the church for some time.

When we exited the church, we noticed there was a small group of people gathered around something. When we drew closer to the circle, we realized that the women who were previously crying were in the center. One was sharing a passionate story, while the other was standing next to her quietly. The older woman who was talking was the mother of the younger woman. We could hear those standing around us and watching saying "Praise be to God!" Suddenly the mother turned to her daughter and said "Show them your stomach, let them see with their own eyes!" I then suddenly heard people exclaiming "Be esm el Saleeb!" (In the name of the Cross!) I thought what they were looking at must have been a burn or some injury, as there were too many people in front of me to see. My mum moved away and found a gap and she also exclaimed "Be esm el Saleeb!" I went to her and asked what she saw while trying to have a look myself, but could see that the lady quickly covered her stomach and was starting to feel uncomfortable. Mum replied "Saleeb! Fe Solban!" (A Cross! There are Crosses!) I was confused, but I watched my mum and uncle approach the mother that was talking and asked politely if she could please repeat the story. The lady enthusiastically exclaimed that her daughter standing next to her was sick with an incurable illness for many years. The family tried everything they could to treat the illness. Eventually as they were losing hope, and started believing that there would be no cure, the lady with the illness decided to ask St. George for his help - she was desperate and really needed a miracle.

This was her last straw of hope, she had tried everything else! The next morning, she woke up and felt different. Something had changed and she couldn't figure out what it was. When she came to get dressed, she felt healthier and more energetic- she had not felt this way for a very long time. She then realized that her stomach was covered with red Crosses. She couldn't believe her eyes and screamed for help! Her mother ran into the room panicking to see what had happened, and was extremely shocked to see her daughter had red Crosses all over her stomach. When the daughter turned around, her mum noticed she had red Crosses all over her back too! They were both in shock, screaming, and praising God. She knew that their prayers had been answered - she was in complete and utter shock. She tried to rub the crosses off but they wouldn't go away, they seemed to be stuck on. She was sure that something extraordinary had happened to her. That day they decided to go to St. George's monastery and thank him for what he did. There was no other possible solution except that St George healed her from her illness and left crosses behind to show her that her prayers had been answered. Many people at the monastery got to witness the red Crosses on her skin, it was something truly amazing.

† † †

I was definitely in shock. I had goosebumps all over my skin. I couldn't believe I got to hear and witness such a wonderful story, right there in front of me! It made me instantly appreciate how holy and special Egypt was. It made me realize how close the saints really are, and how they would love for us to ask for their prayers and intercessions. It was extremely humbling and eye opening and I was so grateful for this experience. It is definitely something I will carry with me for the rest of my life.

Beyond My Wildest Imagination

- Yostina Boktor -

The sheer excitement of going to see the beautiful kids in Egypt deprived me of any sleep that night. We headed to the airport early that morning while struggling to keep our suitcases shut and worried about their weight as we passed through customs. We wanted to give everything we could to the kids, so we prayed as our chunky suitcases miraculously passed through.

We were greeted by a rush of heat, a parade of beeping cars, a distinct but unexplainable atmosphere and the familiar chatter and laughter of the Egyptians. We were home! It was a feeling like no other. What was once a dream was becoming a reality unfolding before our eyes.

The Australians were the first group to touchdown in the motherland. We were escorted from the airport to the place where we would meet fellow youth from around the world and stay for the next few days. The serenity among the palm trees and the pool at our very own resort was enough to allow us to relax and connect with each other before jet lag got the best of us and we dozed off into the night.

† † †

The rays of morning sunlight, the excitement of the arriving youth and the rolling wheels of the suitcases woke us up that morning. The rest of the crew was here! It was time to finally meet our groups who we would be embarking on the rest of our time in Egypt with. They were ones we would Facetime at all hours of the day in order to meet and plan our lessons and activities for the kids of Coptic Orphans – the fatherless – who we would be serving.

Julie, my fellow Sydney roommate, and I quickly got ready while hyping each other up to drown out our nervous excitement before going down to meet the rest of the youth. We were embraced by the Americans, the Canadians and the British. We all seemed to click instantly. It felt so refreshing meeting our brothers and sisters from across the world. With only a few days in Cairo with them, it was hard to go our separate ways to our villages in Upper Egypt where we would serve with our designated groups for the next 3 weeks. My group consisted of Romany, our selfless coordinator, 4 of my favourite Americans: Sandy, Phillip, Ebraam and Mark, my British sister, Clara and myself, an Aussie. I may be biased but I was truly blessed with the best. Our different accents kept things interesting to say the least. We quickly became close and experienced many transformative events together.

We were based in Beni Suef, a beautiful but simple place with the happiest and most generous people I've ever come across. We were hosted by Abouna and his amazing family who served us and did everything in their power to make us feel at home and experience everything we've ever wanted in Egypt. From riding donkeys, milking cows, drinking asab, driving toktoks, farming – this list is endless. Their love was so pure and so unconditional. They are the epitome of Christ's love and what it means to be Christ-like. I could never forget their love, their generosity and their kindness. They taught us so very much.

† † †

A feast was awaiting us as we entered our home for the next 3 weeks. I was so overwhelmed by the instant love that we felt as they welcomed us wholeheartedly. This feast of food was consistent for every meal we had during our stay. After we settled in, we were taken on a quick little tour around the glorious Beni Suef. We visited our classrooms where the lessons would take place and we visited the church nearby. Oh what a beautiful sight! The church was packed with people doing all sorts of activities, and it was only a weekday. There were hymn classes, art classes, classes for those who were differently abled, the blind and the deaf. There was something for everyone. We were embraced with overwhelming love by the kids as we walked into their hymns class. We could feel their excitement as they came running towards us, throwing their arms around us in a big, tight hug. They couldn't contain their joy, giggling and squealing with delight as they squeezed us like they hadn't seen us in ages. It felt as if we were their long-lost friends returning after an eternity. All they wanted to do was take photos and shower us with their love. Laughter filled the air, bouncing off the walls of the church. Their cute little faces beaming and their eyes sparkling with mischief and pure happiness. We couldn't help but embrace them despite our tiredness. Our hearts melted at the sight of their uncontainable excitement. As we stood there, surrounded by those precious, excited kids, I couldn't help but feel incredibly blessed and grateful for the love and warmth they shared with us in that moment. When it was time for us to go, the kids wouldn't let us. When we were finally able to make it into our van, the kids surrounded it and ran with us as we drove out, screaming our names and knocking on our windows. This is how they farewelled us every time we went to visit.

††††

We would visit the church often. It was packed with kids each time and their love and embrace for us would grow more and more each day. It was wonderful seeing the kids at church every night that we would visit. It showed how much the church meant to them and showed me what it means to be immersed in the church. Something I took for granted before.

The next day we woke up nice and early ready to tackle the first day of teaching English and meeting all of our kids! Clara, my incredible partner, and I entered the classroom. We noticed the kids standing back, their expressions shy and guarded. Their hesitant eyes darted towards us, unsure of our presence and intentions. Understanding their apprehension, we approached them gently, giving them space to warm up and feel comfortable. After a few ice breakers and activities they started to come out of their shell a little but were still very guarded. We took them out and played a game called "stuck in the mud," which they called "kahraba." It was incredible to see their faces light up as Clara and I ran around with them. Throughout the next few days we started to see the students become more and more like themselves, their exciting personalities and huge hearts came to life. We were able to connect with them and form strong bonds. It was so amazing to joke around with these kids and see them smiling and having a laugh. For them, their favourite activity was playing outside and chasing each other around as long as Clara and I joined too, that was their rule. Their smiles were infectious, erasing our fatigue and replacing it with their upbeat energy as we entered the gates each morning!

These kids meant so much to us. They taught me so much whilst serving them. I came into this expecting to offer my support and care to these beautiful kids but was taken aback by the humbling experience of the kids showering us with an outpouring of love and kindness. In their innocence, they taught me the true meaning of selflessness and the power of unconditional love. They showed us that kindness knows no boundaries and that even the smallest of acts can have a profound impact; that true service lies not in grand gestures, but in the genuine connections we forge and the love we share with one another.

† † †

To get to know the kids a little more, we were fortunate enough to visit their homes. Visitations occurred after our classes. These were the most memorable for the kids and allowed us to connect better with them as they often felt more comfortable once they shared their story. It was beautiful to see the kids in their homes, with their loved ones. We had lots of fun and played so many games with each of the children in their homes. Some showed us their talents, some opened up about their lives and others were just so happy that we were able to visit them. I was truly touched by the children's mothers. Their spirits emanated warmth and radiated with love, care and unwavering gratitude despite their struggles and hardships. It was eye opening seeing the immense love and faith that they had in Christ. They touched our hearts. We didn't want to leave, and they didn't want to let us go – it was hard leaving each home, but I will forever remember each of them – their radiant smiles and their uplifting spirits.

† † †

We rode the streets of Beni Suef back to church in a different mode of transport every night to keep things interesting. This included a toktok, the back of a ute, a roofless car – anything and everything as we were surrounded by donkeys, cows, carriages and anything else you can imagine in the streets. The streets were energetic and magnetic at all hours of the day and especially at night – the people of Egypt never sleep. The dynamic energy of kids at the church filled us with one more burst of energy before we had to retreat to Abouna's sanctuary – where we stayed.

Every night without fail, Abouna and his family would be awaiting us with open arms and yet another feast. His kids would come running at us and ask, "Yostina ento konto fen" ("Yostina, where were you all"). They would melt our hearts every single time, we were just so so blessed. There were truly not enough hours in the day to spend the amount of time we wished to spend with all the beautiful souls that we had the pleasure of encountering. At times we ended the night, as a group, chatting and debriefing about our jam-packed days.

But most nights we would barely make it to our beds before crashing until the next morning.

†††

The adventures did not stop there! We were so fortunate to be able to travel during the weekends to visit and experience some of the most beautiful churches and monasteries across Egypt which hold a tremendous amount of substance and history that encompass our entity as Coptic Orthodox Christians. One of the places that we visited which resonated with me was Der el Maharraq located in Asyut. This monastery lies exactly in the middle of Egypt which fulfilled the prophesy of Isaiah 19, "there will be an altar of the Lord in the midst of the land of Egypt." Here, the Holy family stayed for 6 months – the longest they have ever stayed in one place in Egypt. Jesus consecrated the altar there Himself, so any new churches built in that area do not need to be consecrated. In this church the Coptic language is the only language used to pray the mass, as a tradition, and a mass is prayed here daily. I loved learning about this monastery and the rich history that it had!

†††

Another place we visited that stood out to me was the monastery of St Mary in Dronka, also located in Asyut. It was believed to be one of the last places the Holy family visited. An extraordinary monastery where you were greeted with a breathtaking mosaic of the Holy family

Beyond My Wildest Imagination

This place is where Anba Youannes prays his annual kiahk praises, which he is famous for, a reason I was so excited to visit! We stayed here over night and some of the most fond memories were shared here with the group. We sang hymns here, Arabic and English, at the top of our lungs and heard it echo through the night.

† † †

We also visited Gabal al-Tayr, in Minya, where the Holy family also visited. It was estimated that Jesus stayed here when he was 3 years old for about 3 months. As the Holy family was sailing through the Nile to the mountain, a rock started to fall. Jesus, at 3 years old, held out his hand and stopped the rock from falling. An imprint of Jesus' tiny hand can still be seen on the rock today. Hence, the mountain was called Gabal al-Kaff (Mountain of the Palm) before it was changed to Gabal et-Tayr (Mountain of Birds). This is because nowadays, unique birds migrate there annually and stay there for the rest of their life.

† † †

Lastly, we were blessed to visit the church of the 21 Martyrs of Libya. Some of their beautiful families came and spoke to us about their husbands, the Martyrs. We were able to see their caskets and their belongings which are displayed in the church for everyone to receive their blessings. This was one of the more emotional visits. But to end we had a few group members get the Coptic

Cross tattooed on their wrists.

† † †

During our last few days in Egypt, many other churches and monasteries were visited when we got back to Cairo with the whole Coptic Orphan's team! And can't forget the pyramids and the camel rides too. It was so great to see everyone again. We all shared our experiences and stories with each other and connected, making more amazing memories together.

Leaving was one of the hardest things to do! Many tears were shed and songs were sung but we await a reunion! It was incredible serving alongside humble, Christ-like people who taught me the true meaning of service.

This trip to Egypt was an immaculate experience. It was truly transformative. One with so many memories made, so many lessons learnt and so many beautiful connections formed. I would not have wanted to do this trip with anyone but our very own 2022 Coptic Orphans crew! I recommend Coptic Orphans, Serve to Learn or a trip to Egypt to all the youth. It is a euphoric experience and I guarantee you that it is one of life's greatest experiences!

An Apple a Day Keeps the Devil Away

- Maria Gindy -

Serve to Learn was one of the most enlightening experiences of my life. While I expected to come out of it with shocking stories to share with friends and family, I found the most significant takeaway for me was the sheer simplicity of the children and families in the program. There was one little girl in particular who gave her heart to me in a way that was so pure and genuine. She and I really bonded over the course of several days in which I taught her class English. She really loved the coloring exercises, and it was clear to me how much she enjoyed our lessons.

One day as she walked in, she told me with pure excitement that she had a gift for me. She pulled out an apple with the largest grin on her face. This truly melted my heart. To the reader, this may sound insignificant.

What may confuse the reader further is the fact that the apple was in fact bruised, and one could say it took a hard fall from the tree. And yet, this gift meant so much to me. Let me tell you why.

Firstly, the undeniable innocence yielded this gift so precious in my sight. In her heart, she truly believed this was the greatest thing she could give me. Her eight-year-old brain had no knowledge of worldly value and riches. She had no idea this gift would be the type that would be laughed at by someone in a different country on Christmas day. Yet, this gift touched my heart in a way no other could. Not to mention, she went out of her way to carry that apple all the way from home. I couldn't help but picture her, with her precious apple in her hand, on a sweaty, crowded bus that picked up children one-by-one from the surrounding village to come to our classroom. All this in anticipation to show her "Miss" from Canada how much she adored her lessons.

This interaction led me to reflect on what I truly perceive as valuable and dear to me. I realized the greatest gifts often have nothing to do with the dollar sign attached to them. Rather, they have more to do with the love one has accumulated from the person giving the gift, rather than the gift itself. This compassion, which is only reflected in a gift, is what truly allows those around us to feel seen and loved. When we pour out our love to those around us, it is communicated in even the smallest of actions and gifts. I think of this like a board in front of the sun's rays. No matter how dark the board may be, the rays of sun still peek behind it and seep through, due to the overwhelming strength of the light. Humans can sense true and authentic love when they receive it. It does not make a difference whether it is wrapped in a shiny box or in a torn plastic bag. And we are called to love deeply and genuinely, as our Father loves us. I hope that one day I can make others feel the same way this eight-year-old girl made me feel when she showed me my Father's love wrapped in a bruised apple, alongside a radiant smile I can never forget.

Boundless Faith

- David Morkos -

Fatigue and a tired voice. That is what I was left with at the end of my English lesson with the students that I served through Coptic Orphans in Aswan, Egypt. However, I was also left with an infinite amount of joy and love. These kids were unlike any Sunday school students I had ever taught back in Australia. They had a different demeanor, they behaved like grown aunts and uncles. What was the reason, I pondered.

It was around lunchtime when we had some lunch, rested, and then one of the local uncles arrived downstairs in a micro-bus. It was time to do some home visitations. A local representative from the church would take us with them to the homes of the children who we taught in the morning. This was my favorite part of the service—home visitations. Especially when one of the boys, Bishoy*, told me in the church playground, "Hat sharfnah el naharda," which means, "We are very excited to have you join us at our home." We arrived at

Gerges* and Bishoy's home. These two were the funniest kids I have ever met. Bishoy, who is around ten years old, worked at the shop of a hairdresser, and Gerges aspired to be a vet. The boys had the most contagious smiles I had ever seen. Our visit alone made their hearts melt. The fact that there were people from Australia, America, and London all visiting the same house was more than enough to give them joy. I cannot express to you the joy and love I had for these kids when we visited them in their homes. It was so pure. These kids were different. They had lost their father figure, so they shouldered many responsibilities at an early age—responsibilities and troubles that no child should experience. The Coptic Orphans Program helps young kids who have lost their father, which means they lost their main source of income. It makes sure that the kids go back to school and pairs them up with people from all across the world to sponsor them each month, which assists them and helps them continue their education.

† † †

In another home visitation, we met a young boy named Matthew*, who is one of four boys. His father passed away in 2011, and it was yet another one of the sweetest visits I had been a part of. It followed a similar pattern - we sat in their presence, and we could see the smiles of his family. His mother, aunt, and their children were all sitting in the same room. It was a very humble home; they didn't have much. However, despite their poverty, they were rich in Christ. Matthew's aunt shared a story with us. Once, she didn't have enough money to pay for her son's tutoring, so the tutor took him out of the lessons. In desperation, the aunt started praying with tears. Moments later, she found an envelope with two hundred pounds placed inside. It made me reflect on the power of faith. How quickly God takes care of His children. I wondered if it was because they had no other solution, no hope, but to rely on their Father in Heaven. Could that be the reason why God answered their prayers so swiftly? They also shared another story about a family that couldn't have any children. They prayed to a particular saint, and miraculously, they bore a son. This faith is the real deal, unlike anything I had witnessed back home.

† † †

Another one of my students, Basant*, a young and quite shy girl, had experienced the loss of both her father and brother. Her family lived in a very small home where the living room could barely accommodate four young adults. They had next to nothing. However, I witnessed a heartwarming moment when Basant's mother gave her some money. Basant left for a moment and returned with a small biscuit and apple juice for each of us. Even though they could barely provide for themselves, they still offered us something to eat and drink. It reminded me of the story of the widow who offered Elijah the last bit of her oil and flour, despite having nothing. This visitation stood out from the rest because Basant, the young girl, wasn't smiling. We tried talking to her, but all our attempts failed. However, there is a glimmer of hope in this story. The program I was serving with is called the Serve to Learn Program, run by Coptic Orphans. The servants in this program spend three weeks in Egypt teaching school kids English. We ask them about their dreams and hopes, and we encourage them to work towards their goals. Throughout the program, I noticed a slight change in Basant's demeanor. She started to smile and tell us jokes. By the end of the trip, I witnessed a small positive change in Aswan. What did we do? We simply sat and ate in their presence. That simple act was enough to bring a smile to one person's face.

It is indeed fascinating. Prior to my trip to Egypt, I held great anticipation to witness a miracle, but instead, I encountered something distinct and extraordinary. I witnessed the Bible coming to life before my eyes. Faith, love, and hope manifested themselves through the families we visited. Observing their unwavering faith and profound love for God was the true miracle. These families demonstrated a complete reliance on God, as they had no one else to turn to. And it was remarkable to see how God heard and answered their heartfelt prayers, blessing them abundantly.

† † †

During one of our final visitations, we encountered

wonderful kids living in an extremely impoverished home. Their living room served as their bedroom, kitchen, and laundry room. As we boarded the bus to return home, many questions came to my mind. Why was I blessed with such a luxurious life in Australia while my brothers and sisters in Egypt were enduring hardship? It wasn't their fault. None of us choose where we are born. Visiting Egypt and serving these blessed children instilled in me a deep sense of gratitude and a profound realization that I must find ways to help these children, whether through sponsorship, prayer, or by serving anyone in need. It also taught me the transformative power of home visitations, and the impact that can be made simply by being present in someone's life. It reaffirmed the truth found in the scripture, "For where two or three are gathered in my name, I am there among them" (Matthew 18:20).

*For the sake of privacy, the names of the individuals in the story have been changed to Bishoy, Gerges, Matthew and Basant, appearing throughout the stories in this order.

Scan the QR code to go to our website where you will find

- Book reviews
- Great deals
- Our full library of books

www.ingramcontent.com/pod-product-compliance
Lightning Source LLC
Chambersburg PA
CBHW070321100426
42743CB00011B/2501

* 9 7 8 0 6 4 5 7 7 0 3 6 0 *